St. Mary Magdalen, Oxford.

30 August 1976

Jim Charles,
St. Edmund Hall,
Oxford

65p

20 p
SALE

D1741859

LIVING WITH GOD

LIVING WITH GOD

An Introduction to the
Practice of Prayer

BY

E. W. TRUEMAN DICKEN

LONDON
SPCK

First published 1957
A. R. Mowbray & Co. Ltd
The Alden Press
Osney Mead
Oxford OX2 0EG

Second edition 1975
SPCK
Holy Trinity Church
Marylebone Road
London NW1 4DU

Printed Offset in Great Britain by
W. Hart and Son Ltd
(incorporating The Talbot Press)
Saffron Walden, Essex

ISBN 0 281 02853 2

AUTHOR'S NOTE

This book consists basically of the material given in three Lenten broadcasts in the Midland Home Service of the B.B.C. in 1956. The original scripts were largely recast and rearranged for publication, and a considerable amount of new material was added.

In the present (second) edition a few further improvements and corrections have been made and some passing allusions brought up to date. Otherwise the text remains unchanged from the first edition.

CONTENTS

LIVING WITH GOD

I

THE ROYAL PRESENCE

Why should we trouble ourselves to pray? Most people don't pray and are not noticeably the worse for it. Does it matter whether we pray or not?

It is a crucial question, and much of this book will be an attempt to answer it; but we must have at least a rough-hewn answer to the problem from the outset. We cannot pray unless we understand something of the purpose of prayer. So let us look at the facts first of all.

We live in the world which God has made, and if we are going to live at all we can't escape from it, or from Him. We are a part of His design, and He evidently wants us here or He would not have put us here. If a man designs something—a motor car, for instance—he does it with a purpose in mind. He knows what each part of it is for and how it works, and he doesn't put in gears or wires or switches which serve no useful purpose. If we use the car in the way he intended, all the parts will work and we shall get results.

Of course, when we buy a car there may be a good deal about it we don't understand. If we misuse it, whether intentionally or through ignorance, it will not be surprising if we put it out of order. We must run the car according to the maker's instructions if we want to drive about in it, and then it will take us wherever there is a road.

Equally, we can try living in God's world any way we please, since to a greater or lesser extent we all have free will. But if we want to make anything worth while of living in the world, we must follow God's instructions. There can be no other way.

A car manufacturer gives you a handbook to tell you how your car works and how to look after it, and God has given us a handbook of His world—the Bible. We can't manage without it any more than the man who maintains his own car can manage without the maker's handbook.

The really keen motorist isn't even content just to read the handbook. He keeps his knowledge fresh and up-to-date by reading a motoring magazine and technical books; and the Christian needs to keep himself in the picture by reading modern books about Christians and Christianity, the weekly religious press and the Book of Common Prayer itself. The more we read, the better equipped we shall be for the job of living in God's world.

But God is much more personal, much more interested in us than any car manufacturer is in his vehicles. It is not enough for us simply to know *about* Him. Even a mechanic needs more than merely technical skill: he needs to know his employer, and his employer's personal likes and dislikes. And we need to know *God*, by direct personal contact. There's only one way of doing it. We must be *with* God, consciously and intentionally with Him, which is what we call, in one word, prayer.

In fact, then, prayer is quite indispensable to all of us, because we all work for God, whether we like it or not. He made us, and we cannot alter that situation. What is more, we ought not to want to alter it. God is not only very much more personal than any car manufacturer or employer: He is both our Creator and our Father.

In a human family, nothing can alter the fact that a man or a boy is the son of his father, and a good father still cares about his son, however much of a black sheep he may turn out to be. God is the perfect Father, no less; and He will not send us away or refuse to help us if we fall short of His plans for us. He will go on doing all He can for us—all that we will let Him do for us, in fact—as long as we live.

We human beings are so obstinate and self-centred ourselves that we find that very difficult to grasp, but it should give us every possible incentive to keep close to God. We have everything to gain from the contact. How are we to set about making it?

We have all tried praying at one time or another. Some of us have made a regular habit of it for years. Some have tried it for a time and then given it up. Some have prayed just two or three times in their lives—in a crisis, perhaps, or in a moment of intense fear or distress. At least we have all had some experience of prayer.

Have you personally found prayer much of a success? Many people haven't, even among those who pray regularly. The trouble is, very often, that they have rather lost sight of what prayer is, and of what it is for. Perhaps they were told as children that, 'Praying means talking to God' and have found the process rather a one-sided conversation. When one thinks of it, one realizes that however helpful that definition may be to children, it isn't strictly accurate, and to an adult it can be more of a hindrance than a help. Praying is simply *being*, quite consciously and intentionally, *with God*.

Two young people who are in love can be together by the hour enjoying each other's company without saying a word; and the less we prattle at God when we are with Him in our prayers, the better our prayers are likely to be. Père de Caussade says in his great treatise 'On Prayer':

'We must rid ourselves of the error of numbers of people who do not think that they are praying unless they are in continuous movement, piling reflection on reflection, prayer on prayer, act on act. We must banish this super-fluity for the principal part, the attention of the heart (of which most people rarely think). Yet without this atten-tion, vocal prayers will never be more than a vain noise of words, and meditation and reading will be pure amuse-ment of the mind.'

What, in fact, for most of us spoils our chance of praying well is that, right at the outset, we approach the matter from a false angle. Just think what it really means to come to our prayers. We are coming into the presence of the Lord of all creation. This attention of the heart that de Caussade speaks of means, then, first and foremost that we must be respectful.

Have you ever tried to get an interview with your local M.P.? It isn't very easy as a rule. Senior civil servants are even less accessible, and you could wait a lifetime for a private interview with the Prime Minister. Yet just for the trouble of kneeling down you can have the undivided attention of the King of kings, God Almighty, for as long as you wish. God isn't limited to time and space like us. He can, so to speak, spend all eternity just listening to your prayers, and still have all eternity for everybody else.

Being, as He is, a loving Father, He is prepared to listen, but if we should take care to prepare properly for an interview with an important human being, we shall realize what care we must take over an audience with God.

St. Ignatius Loyola gives this advice: when you are going to pray, don't start at once by kneeling down. Start by standing silently for a moment, and remind yourself that, when you kneel, it will be like entering the throne room of the heavenly King. Don't rush into His presence hot and panting from the last job you were doing, or with the idea that you can only spare a few minutes with Him anyway. Think how you would conduct yourself before earthly Royalty, waiting very diffidently upon their pleasure.

'We should make our petition,' says the Spanish mystic, St. Teresa of Avila, 'like beggars before a powerful and rich Emperor; then, with downcast eyes, humbly wait. Our Lord wishes us at such a time to offer Him our petitions and to place ourselves in His presence. He knows what is best for us.'

We are to remember, in fact, that we do not come before God as equals for a pleasant discussion. We do not even come to Him as to a wise counsellor who will give us good advice. We come before Him as Lord of all, the One who knows all and who, in His infinite wisdom, can never be mistaken or misled.

We can come to almost any one of our friends to ask advice, and when they have given their opinion, we can take it or leave it. We cannot do that with God. We cannot ask His advice. We can only ask for His commands.

We must realize, though, that the action of God's Holy Spirit is almost unbelievably gentle. God won't argue with us. If He did, His almighty power would simply crush us, and that is not His purpose. So unless we come to obey, we shall simply get nothing at all out of our prayers. Why should we expect to? We are not doing God a favour in praying to Him; we are receiving the greatest favour a human being can receive.

As we should expect, God is Himself quite the best teacher of prayer, but at the same time there is practically no-one who does not need outside help from time to time. It is one of the difficulties in writing about prayer that no two people are ever at precisely the same stage of spiritual development; and no two people pray in exactly the same

B

way, because every human being is unique and God deals with each one of us individually. No book on prayer can ever give you tailor-made answers to your own personal problems in prayer, however much it may help in a general way.

The safe rule is that, if you are already in the habit of praying regularly, and seem to be doing something worth while in your prayers, you should not let anyone persuade you to do anything different. Keep on as you are. Make changes gradually, and expect to learn only by trial and error. The Church has hammered out its teaching on prayer through centuries of hardly-won experience, and these pages aim to say only what the Church has said throughout the ages. One's best hope of learning to pray well lies in relying upon the Church's experience rather than in following what seem to be bright, new ideas and which are probably tawdry old ones which the Church long ago investigated and found to be blind alleys. But if advice from anyone, however good the authority, seems to be wrong *for you* at the time, just pay no attention to them. The advice may be appropriate to someone else's case, and perhaps will fit you, too, in years to come; but don't try to make alterations in a hurry as long as your prayers are going well.

At the same time, we must be prepared to learn in our prayers, however good they are now. What is right for us now may be quite wrong in a few years' time. It is quite pitiful to be told by people that they don't seem to be able to pray properly any more, and then to find out that they are still trying, perhaps in middle age, to say the same prayers that they were taught at their mother's knee or learned in their confirmation classes.

A middle aged man would look very silly trying to wear the clothes he had as a schoolboy, and it would be quite grotesque if he hadn't any other clothes to wear at all! It is even worse if he tries to cling on to the prayers he knew as a small boy, or to the way of praying he learned years ago. His soul goes on growing (that is, his personality goes on maturing) long after his body has ceased to change much. We soon outgrow our prayers, even quite late in life, if we don't make an effort to learn more and more about the job of praying year by year.

We must never, then, bring to our prayers that frame of mind which 'won't be told.' Everything about our prayers must be done in a humble and obedient attitude. We must never be guilty of the impertinence of *demanding* anything of God, not even better prayers! He is too infinitely far above us for that. We must put ourselves in His hands with the confidence of a small child, and prepare to follow His wishes, however difficult they may be.

Spend a minute or two at least when you first start your prayers thinking over what your attitude to God ought to be. Realize how infinitely loving He is, and how very little we have to offer Him. Think how quite incomprehensibly powerful He is, the Maker and Controller of the whole vast universe, and how abysmally tiny and insignificant we are. Recognize the fact that all His wishes are perfect, and that we are almost hopelessly foolish and ill-behaved.

If you do nothing else in the whole of your prayer-time but just this, you will have made the very best possible use of it.

2

THE VALUE OF HABIT

To pray is a natural human activity. Anyone can pray. Everyone ought to pray. And absolutely no-one can get along properly without praying. Yet is is very common for people to say, 'I do *want* to pray, but I simply can't. I think I'm probably not a very spiritual sort of person.' They are making the mistake of thinking that a Christian is someone altogether out of this world, one of those people whose feet are planted firmly in mid-air.

Now, one can think of a good many Christians who are like that, but that is simply because they are not such good Christians as they might be. Our Lord was thoroughly down-to-earth. So were His apostles; and if we want to pray, *we* have got to see things, including ourselves, as they really are, too.

We aren't by nature heavenly creatures. We are of the earth, earthy, even though we have a heavenly destiny. God did not create us as angels, and the Church has never taught that He did. Read the story of creation at the very beginning of the Bible, and you will see that it is not, at bottom, saying anything very different from what modern scientists are beginning to discover. Mankind (Adam, that is, in the biblical text) was formed out of the dust of the ground. Put in present-day language, it means this : human beings are basically made up of all the animal and vegetable matter they eat, which comes from the soil in the first place. We are strictly, as the Book of Genesis says, just dust of the earth—dirt and water.

When we die, our bodies will turn back into dust again. The one thing which distinguishes us from dust is that we have life, that factor which God alone can supply. Vegetables have life of a sort, and animals have life of a rather higher sort because they have instincts and a certain freedom of movement. Human beings have life of a still higher category, because they have intelligence and free will. But that does not make us angels.

We talk a good deal about human souls from time to time, but often we have no very clear idea of what we mean by the word 'soul.' The modern word which perhaps comes nearest to explaining what it means, or ought to mean if we use it properly, is 'personality.' May we please forget anything we have ever heard about God having a collection of souls in heaven which He attaches to the bodies of human babies when they are born? The Church very early recognized that as a false view. Our personality is something which did not exist at all before our conception, and which grows and develops along with our bodies.

A tiny baby has not very much intelligence, nor has it very much personality. It lives largely by instinct, just as an animal does. It drinks it's mother's milk without knowing why, but that is what keeps it alive and makes it grow until it can begin to understand the world for itself. Gradually the child's instincts give way to habits, the difference being that habits have to be learned by training, conscious or unconscious. Instincts seem to be just a part of the nature of animals, human or quadruped, and, of course, remain with us more or less all our lives.

Personality begins to develop still later on, at least in any noticeable degree. It is not easy to define it, but it has a good deal to do with *purpose*. A man with personality is a man with purpose—a purpose in life as a whole, and with purpose in everything he does. He impresses us simply because he isn't flabby or easily knocked down. He sees a thing and goes for it, and his whole make-up gives us an impression of definiteness and strength and reliability.

Personality is, in fact, very much bound up with free will. A man whose choice of action is governed by an overriding purpose is a man of personality, and personality is least evident in those who are feeble and easily diverted from their object. We may say, then, that a man's soul is something which grows from his having a body, a living body directed by intelligent free will which he applies to his actions. But fundamentally he is still no more than an animated clay figure, made by God and given life by Him for a specific purpose.

All this has a very direct bearing upon prayer. In the first place, it helps us to get a right attitude to ourselves when we come into God's presence. When we remember that we are no more than dust and ashes, we realize that many of the things we commonly say to God are rank impertinence. He is our Maker, and a Being of a quite different order from ourselves. We are just things that He has made, and we cannot even begin to tell Him how He ought to deal with us.

Secondly, if we bear in mind that we still retain most of the characteristics of the lower animals, however far our minds and souls develop, we shall understand that we have to learn things in much the same way that animals learn them: by continual repetition, by habit, and by continually making a fresh start when we forget what we have learnt before. We are all alike in this, and the need for habit and repetition is as great in learning to pray as it is in cooking the family meals or improving one's game of golf.

It is quite true, no doubt, that any human being can pray after a fashion, anywhere at any time; but if we want to pray well, we have to learn the job. It is not easy, and it takes time. A whole lifetime will not be too long for most of us.

The French writer on the spiritual life, Chénart, states the matter most graphically. He writes:

'Let us persevere constantly in standing at the palace gate of this great Monarch; let us bear ourselves humbly in His divine presence, assured that He sees and watches us. Let us count ourselves over-honoured in being admitted to stand before Him, though we cannot say a word. Let us think ourselves thrice happy if after many hours, days, months or years we can perform some small duty for Him, obtain a look, a word, a good thought or movement from Him. Let us not be astonished if we do badly at prayer and are distracted at the beginning. If we willingly spend several years acquiring the mechanical arts or learning some humane science, how could we wish to be masters in a few days of the exercise of prayer, which is the art of arts and the science of the saints? How long have we been practising prayer? With what perseverance have we done so? What care have we taken to instruct ourselves in the means of success? What have we done to obtain from God so great a gift as the spirit of prayer? What sacrifice, what austerity, what penance have we undergone to attain it? .... When we have persevered for many years in these practices, and even for our whole life, we shall not even then have cause for complaint; for God owes to no-one this extraordinary gift of prayer. He gives it to whom He pleases. ... Let us persevere and ask unceasingly for this precious gift of prayer; the desire itself will be an excellent prayer that God will not fail to hear.'

Clearly, on Chénart's showing, the first stage in learning to pray is to form good habits. We need regular practice, and we shall not get it unless we make a regular time for praying each day. A child learning to play the piano or the violin is expected to practice for at least half an hour every day. It does not seem unreasonable to ask an adult to spend at least twenty minutes a day learning to pray. When you think of it, it is not even polite to God to give Him less of your time than you spend in reading the daily paper.

I do not suggest that you should give this twenty minutes to prayer all at the same time. It will be much more valuable if you spend, say, five minutes in the morning when you first get up, five minutes at night before you go to bed, and the remaining ten minutes (preferably more) at some other time during the day when you can be on your own, quietly, for a little while. The essential is that these times shall become a habit, because good habits are almost as hard to break as bad ones, and if you fix a definite time or stage in your day when you habitually come to your prayers, you will have your habits working *for* you instead of against you.

You will help to fasten this habit if you not only make a regular time of day for your prayers, but also a regular place. It isn't easy to put gardening and cooking and T.V. and money and worry out of one's head at a moment's notice, but if you have a definite place to which you come to be with God, it does help to impress upon you what you have come there for. William Law, writing in the eighteenth century, puts it like this :

'If you were to use yourself (as far as you can) to pray always in the same place; if you were to reserve that place for devotion, and not allow yourself to do anything common in it; if you were never to be there yourself but in times of devotion; if any little room, or (if that cannot be) if any particular part of a room were thus used, this kind of consecration of it, as a place holy unto God, would have such an effect upon your mind....as would very much assist your devotion. For by having a place thus

sacred in your room, it would in some measure resemble a
chapel or house of God. This would dispose you to be
always in the spirit of religion when you were there.
Your own apartment would raise in your mind such
sentiments as you have when you stand near an altar,
which is the place of prayer and holy intercourse with
God.'

Sadly, in these days of prevalent vandalism, few churches
are able to be left permanently unlocked; but if you are
fortunate enough to live or work near a church which is
open during the day, here is an excellent place for prayer.
Its very atmosphere will help you to pray. To drop in for
ten minutes or a quarter of an hour at lunch time or on your
way home or while you are out shopping can be unbelievably refreshing to the body as well as the spirit.

This matter of atmosphere is a very important one.
There are places in which it is not easy to remember that
God is present. He is everywhere, of course, but if we
cannot grasp the fact, then it will be more difficult to
pray. We need to be, so to speak, 'at home' in our prayers.
We know, perhaps only too well, how a child will do
things in someone else's house which it would not dream
of doing at home. We are likely to spend our prayer time
better for being in a spot where we are 'at home,' because
it helps us to follow our good habits.

In our own room a picture of our Lord or a crucifix
hung on the wall can add immeasureably to the atmosphere, and keep our mind on what we are there for. In a
church many people find it a great help to recollection to
pray kneeling before the Blessed Sacrament.

A small point worth mentioning is that it is often better
not to shut our eyes when we pray. Children are usually
told to shut their eyes to keep out the sight of things which
distract their attention, but most adults have far too lively

imaginations for that to be necessarily the best way of concentrating. Sometimes it is, but often shutting our eyes merely sets us off thinking about everything under the sun, just as it does when we can't get to sleep in the middle of the night. At times like that a crucifix or a small statue of our Lord or of our Lady can be a great asset.

It also helps our concentration if we make a rule of always kneeling to pray. The attitude of our body is nearly always closely bound up with our attitude of mind, and just as a respectful workman does not slouch with his hands in his pockets when he addresses his employer, so the Christian will be likely to make a more reverent approach to God if he kneels. It is the natural position of humble obedience.

It is not a good idea to lean against furniture, especially against our bed, to pray. The bed is so cosy and warm and inviting that it puts half our mind to sleep at once, and makes the other half eager to follow suit as soon as possible! Kneeling upright takes rather more effort, of course, but it does keep one alert and respectful. Discomfort or mere idleness are no excuse for discourtesy to our superiors even in this world.

If you really cannot remain kneeling for long enough, then try standing for a change. We are accustomed to standing when important people come into the room, and again the same action can remind us of the honour due to God. Sitting is, for most of us, the least helpful of all positions. We cannot help knowing in the back of our minds that we are putting our comfort before God's glory.

In the end, of course, it is our attitude of mind which matters; but we need to be sufficiently humble not to despise simple ways of overcoming the limitations of our animal nature.

Of course, there is a point at which habits can become a danger. Habit should serve our prayers, not dictate them. In particular we need to watch that the very words we use in our prayers are not a hindrance to us. It is very common to find that people who bring an altogether right and devout attitude of mind to their prayers are almost hopelessly cramped by the fact that they know only five or six prayers by heart and do not seem to be able to get away from them.

If we use prayers out of a book or prayers which we know by heart, then we must be sure that they are prayers which we can say sincerely, prayers which we really *mean*. Prayers we used as children, apart from the Lord's Prayer, do not usually mean much to an adult, and we need new prayers and thanksgivings to match the different situations we meet as our circumstances change. Far better to scrap the set prayers altogether and say what we mean to God in our own words, however haltingly, than to be tied to a habit of incomplete sincerity.

It is worth remembering, though, that in the courts of earthly kings there is a fairly strict code of etiquette about forms of address, just as there is in law courts or parliament. Those forms of address are designed to remind us of the dignity of those we are addressing; and the time-hallowed forms of address to God as 'Lord God Almighty,' 'Lord of lords, King of kings,' 'Almighty and most merciful Father' and so on all serve to inculcate a right attitude on the part of those who use them.

The test of all prayer ultimately, of course, is whether it is sincere. Whatever words we use, we must *be ourselves*. What is more, we must be prepared to let God see us as we are. We have to become the sort of people whose lives are fit to be an open book, and who don't mind who inspects it. Bishop Jeremy Taylor, the great Caroline divine, put it most succinctly: 'Be a whole man, all of a piece.' The advice I have ventured to give about making our body, mind and soul all work together in our prayer time should be part of a process which infiltrates all our other activities. We are made aware of the Royal Presence on our knees so that we may be aware of it all the time. Every aspect of our personality must be brought into line with our main purpose in life, which is to serve God's purpose with our whole self in everything that we do.

3
REQUESTS AND REQUISITES

IF we wish to make any real progress in our prayers it will be much better, as we have seen, if instead of using prayers out of a book which often we don't really mean, we pray to God in our own words. That, of course, presents a real difficulty to most people. They tend to use a book or prayers which they know by heart simply because they do not know what to say otherwise. They become tongue-tied, largely because they are not at all confident that they know the right sort of things to say to God.

Well, what do we *want* to say?

Being human, I am afraid that most of us find it easiest in our prayers to *ask* for things. It is not the highest form of prayer, but there is nothing to be ashamed of in it provided that we are not just being selfish in our asking. If we can manage to ask God quite easily and without embarrassment in our own words for the things we need, then we may gradually acquire the habit of bringing everything to Him, all our fears and ambitions and worries and hopes and wants. There is, after all, nothing we cannot tell God.

I have stressed a good deal the reverence which we owe to God, as Lord of all creation; but we should never lose sight of the fact that He is our Father, that He has condescended with infinite love and generosity to treat us as His own children. Our children do not need a phrase-book to tell them what to say to us! Perhaps if we look for a moment at what it really means to say that God is our Father, we shall see more clearly what there is to pray about.

In the first place, we need to remember that God, like a perfect earthly father (if one can imagine such a person) will stick at absolutely nothing for our good. People who try to pray often feel that God must have deserted them when things go wrong. He hasn't. He never does. Most emphatically, God *always* answers our prayers. If we think otherwise, it is because we are forgetting that there can be at least two answers to every request, 'Yes' and 'No.' God's answer to our prayers frequently must be, 'No' or, perhaps, 'Wait and see.' As St. Augustine says, 'When God does not give us what we wish, it is in order to give us what we would love more if we knew all things.' Sometimes He lets us take a hard knock, and we hate it; but it *is* for our ultimate good, and it *is* the best possible answer to our prayer.

Any parent will let a child have its own misguided way at times, so that it may see for itself the results of its naughtiness or silliness. If we grown-ups pray hard enough and long enough, we too may sometimes get our own way, only to discover that what we wanted is a very bitter fruit.

We can never afford to forget, indeed, that God is a person—an incalculably more complete and wise person than any of us, but still a person. He isn't like a slot machine into which you put a coin and always get the same result. He treats us as persons, too, and deals with us differently according to different circumstances. His love is constant, but it shows itself in different ways, as our love for our children does.

If we are teaching a tiny child to walk, we hold him up and take extreme care that he doesn't fall and hurt himself. One nasty bump may discourage him for weeks. He may even hurt himself badly and do himself a lasting injury. But a tousle-headed young ruffian of seven or eight is quite a different proposition. When he falls and takes the skin off his knees, we point out firmly that he must learn to be less wild in his behaviour. If we mollycoddle him he will never learn anything of the sort.

So God's answers to our prayers are designed to meet our needs. When He allows us to fall, the most adult way of meeting the situation is to recognize that it *is* for our good, ultimately. God doesn't treat us severely for fun, any more than a good earthly father would.

The Lord's Prayer puts all this very neatly when it says, 'Our Father, ... give us this day our daily bread.' We are to ask God for what we need without any false embarrassment. He is our Father, and He expects to provide for us. At the same time, it's bread He provides mostly, not caviar. He wants us to have healthy bodies and souls, not pampered ones. He also wants us to rely on Him from day to day. It would be extremely bad for us to have such a supply of anything that we felt independent of God: we should soon forget Him altogether.

But may I draw attention particularly to a further point about this phrase from the Lord's Prayer? It does not say, 'Give *me* this day *my* daily bread,' but 'Give *us* this day *our* daily bread—not only myself but everyone else as well as myself.' It is a most important point. Our prayers on behalf of other people ought always to take precedence over our petitions to God for our own worldly, material needs.

Most people have already some notion of this. At all events they like to have someone praying for them, even if they are not so eager to pray for others.

What good does it do to pray for other people? One thing it does not do, and which we ought not to want it to do, is to cajole God—much less bully Him—into doing something He did not intend to do. Occasionally we feel very bitterly about God because He seems unwilling to help someone whom we believe He ought to help. We cannot avoid the feeling that either God is very hard-hearted, or else much less powerful than He is reputed to be. Oddly enough, we are often more ready to accept God's refusal of something we want for ourselves than of something we want for other people. We seem to think that we have to put God under an obligation by un-selfishly praying for someone else's good.

When we find ourselves thinking in this way, do let us try to remember that God is the Creator and Father of the person we are praying for, just as He is our own Creator and Father. However much we may think we care for another person, our thought for them and our prayers for them do not take up much of our time propor-tionately. Yet God has cared for them twenty-four hours a day, three hundred and sixty five days a year, ever since He first made them. It is astoundingly pre-sumptuous of us to think that because we have suddenly decided to take an interest in them, God ought at once to defer to our views. He knows so much better than we do, and He is doing everything possible to help the person we are praying for—everything, that is to say, that the person concerned will let Him do. We can all prevent God helping us if we wish!

It is a sorry thought, but actually we are all of us concerned, most of our time, not to let God interfere with our lives. We want to run them our own way, and we quite intentionally shut God out. He has given us the ability to do that, or, as we usually put it, He has given us *free will*. His only alternative, presumably, would have been to make us puppets, who did exactly what He made us do without any life or love or personality at all. We should be mere things and not people.

Now God evidently cannot take away our free will without spoiling His handiwork in us, killing us and turning us into zombies or robots. What then can He do about people who will not do things His way? He can do this: He can let other human beings influence them. One man cannot take away the free will of another, but in various ways he can influence him profoundly; and prayer for him, 'intercession' as it is called, is the most fundamentally effective of all these ways, as well as being one of the greatest privileges God has to offer us.

Consider: we humans are all individuals, but we are also members of a family, of a nation, a trade, a profession, a club, a social class and so on. We cannot get away from one another. We fit together like the pieces of an intricate jig-saw puzzle, and indeed a very large proportion of our effort in this life is spent in trying to fit ourselves into the right place in this jig-saw.

Now if you lose one piece of a jig-saw puzzle, the other nine hundred and ninety-nine pieces are at once very much less useful. Anyone who looks at the whole picture sees that it is spoilt for want of that one piece. What is perhaps less easy to see, but is equally true, is that the value of every other single piece is affected by the loss of the one missing piece. A spoilt puzzle has only a tenth of the value of a whole one, in terms of sheer hard cash, and it is a matter of simple arithmetic that each separate piece is worth correspondingly less.

Now if these lifeless bits of wood or cardboard affect one another so profoundly, it is not difficult to see how much more profoundly human beings, with their infinitely complex relationships, affect one another. One cannot easily explain how, but two facts stand out very clearly: first, God has promised that it shall be so; secondly, all experience shows that it *is* so.

C

In one sense, although there is much more to it than this, our Lord's life and death can be seen as the supreme example of intercession. God became man in order that He might be able to work on the human race from their side of the great gulf which divides God from man, Master from slave, the Maker from what He has made. As a man, He could do for men what as God and only God He could not do: He could alter their situation and their circumstances without destroying or taking away their freedom of will. His perfect submission to God completed, as it were, the otherwise spoilt and incomplete picture of the human jig-saw.

In interceding for others, in fact, we are actually being allowed to do God's work for Him, sharing the task of our Lord Himself. The blessed John of Ruysbroeck, one of the greatest masters of prayer of all time, puts it this way:

'The man of prayer shall go out towards all men of good will, and shall taste and behold how that they are tied and bound together in love; and he shall beseech and pray God that He may let his customary gifts flow forth, that thereby all may be confirmed in His love and His eternal worship. This man shall faithfully and discreetly serve all men, for he bears in him a love towards all. And thus he is a mediator between God and all men.'

Those who are experienced in prayer sometimes find intercession peculiarly difficult, but comparative beginners, oddly enough, often find it one of the easier kinds of prayer. It gives them a familiar subject to deal with: the obvious needs of men and women and children they know personally.

If you are one of those who finds prayer difficult, then, do set about your intercessions with a fresh heart. You will not need a book to help you. Simply recall to your mind as you pray the people you live with, work with, meet during the day. Quite humbly ask God to help them as He sees fit. Add to your list those who especially seem to need prayers—the sick, the homeless, the hungry, the lonely, the dying. Be imaginative. The bus driver as you go to work, the girl who serves you in the canteen, the operator who answers your telephone—they all need prayers. Your prayers. If your list grows too long to cope with, split it into seven parts, one for each day of the week, and only remember daily those who are particularly close to you. Above all bear in mind that the important matter is not what we want, nor what they want, but what God wants. It is always the very best one can possibly have, and we should be most foolish to pray for anything less good. Again, John of Ruysbroeck puts us on the right lines:

'The man of prayer shall descend towards his fellow sinners with great compassion and with generous mercy, and shall bring them before God with fervent devotion and much prayer; bringing to God's remembrance all the good which He is, and all His power, and all that He has done for us, and has promised us, right as though He has forgotten all this: for God wills that we beseech Him. And charity shall obtain all that it desires; nevertheless, it must not be stubborn or self-willed, but must leave all to the rich goodness and generosity of God: for God loves without measure.'

The primary rule of intercession, as of any other kind of prayer, is to persevere. Whether you can see any results or whether you can't, you can be certain that God will not allow your prayer to go unheeded. It is His work that you are doing. It cannot possibly fail, so do not lose heart.

4
A RIGHT RELATIONSHIP

A GOOD many people who would like to pray don't pray because they feel in all honesty that they cannot. They will say frankly that they have never bothered very much about God, and now when they feel the need of Him, they would be ashamed to start saying their prayers. After all, if you have carefully avoided speaking to your next door neighbour for twenty years, you cannot very well go and ask him to lend you his car for the week-end. You would be ashamed to do it; and so, too, many people are ashamed to start saying their prayers.

One must sympathize a great deal with people in this position. To start to pray in such circumstances may seem almost contemptible if you put it like that. But then one should not put it like that! God is not our next door neighbour. He is our Father and our King. He commands us to pray to Him at all times, and obedience to His command is always better than disobedience, whatever our original motive for making the change. However much a person may give God cause to be angry by never praying to Him, the situation will never be improved by continuing to ignore Him.

If we feel it rather humiliating to come to Him just because we want something, it will be very good for us. We deserve to eat humble pie for our past disobedience, and we shall be the more grateful to God for taking us in on those terms. Perhaps we shall feel the more obliged to go on praying to Him when He has accepted us, if only for shame at the thought of deserting Him again when He no longer seems to be immediately necessary to us.

Do not be afraid that God will not have you. We may
be too proud to come to Him, but He is not too proud to
come to us. 'Him that cometh unto me I will in no wise
cast out,' said Christ, and He lived and died to show that
He meant every syllable of it.

To put the case rather crudely, God is always prepared
to be on good terms with us. The trouble is that we are
not always prepared to be on good terms with Him. We
want to live our lives in our own way, and that makes it
very difficult to have an easy or straightforward relationship with God. We are like a son who disobeys his
father: he cannot ask for favours until he has said he is
sorry, and has been forgiven for his disobedience.

God, unlike human fathers, is so immeasurably loving
that He forgives us absolutely anything. It isn't that He
doesn't care how appallingly we behave. Quite the
contrary, He loves us too deeply to want us to spoil our
lives by even the least imperfection. He may have to
punish us severely at times, but He never punishes us out
of spite or simply to retaliate. He acts at all times for our
good, to save us from ourselves, and He can only do that
by being always ready to forgive. The barrier to good
relations with God is always one of our making, never
of His. What is needed on our side is a change of heart,
a fresh attitude of mind. The Bible calls it repentance.

Now since prayer is essentially the means by which we
establish relations with God, penitence is obviously a
very important part of it. This does not mean, of course,
that Christianity has a morbid preoccupation with sin.
One might as well say that a man who goes to the dentist
to have a decayed tooth extracted has a morbid preoccupation with tooth-ache. The Christian is concerned
with sin just so far as is necessary in order to get rid of it,
and no further. We all sin, just as we all get dirty; and it

is only the incorrigible who refuse to wash.

It is no surprise, then, to find that the Church is full of people who are sinners and who admit it. A hospital is full of people who know they are ill, but they are there to get well, and no-one would say that it is a morbid thing to have hospitals in the world. They are essential to health; and penitence is essential to goodness and godliness.

Human nature, of course, is quite incredibly stubborn in this matter. The vast majority of us are quite unwilling to admit ever having done anything wrong. Even at the point of death, knowing that they have only a few hours in which to make amends, people will continue to insist that they have lived blamelessly. Even those with the most sordid histories of malice and immorality and dishonesty will claim that they have never done any harm to anybody or said anything to be ashamed of.

The clergy are used to hearing this sort of thing, but next door neighbours and friends would often be quite speechless if they knew how altogether oblivious of their own true nature most people are. Take heed! Most of us are in very much the same class. Human nature strongly resents criticism, even self-criticism.

The starting point for all penitence, then, is to admit that one *is* a sinner, because we all are, and from that point to go on to discover in what ways that sinfulness comes out. We call the process 'self-examination,' and it is quite a skilled job. We have to learn the art of penetrating our own defences.

Be warned, it will not be a pleasant experience! But we shall never make much progress unless we do carry out a more or less detailed examination of our conscience every day, preferably towards the end of the day.

If you have one of those little prayer-books with a list of sins to help you to check up on yourself, you will be well advised not to use it except as a last resort. Such lists are very common and popular, but they can often have a thoroughly undesirable influence. We may use them satisfactorily for a few weeks, but once we get used to them one of two results usually follows. Either we decide that we are guilty of every single sin in the list, and that we must be quite hopelessly depraved; or, more probably, we go to the opposite extreme, believe that we have done nothing but what is pleasing to God because the list doesn't seem to catch us out, and congratulate ourselves upon our virtue.

Quite certainly neither point of view will be even faintly justified. None of us is hopeless, and none of us approaches sanctity after a few months or even years of beginners' books on prayer. It is humiliating but salutary to realize that even as a sinner one is merely mediocre.

Self-examination should start with running through in one's mind the events of the past day. What things are there in it which we wish we hadn't done? What things are we ashamed of? What actions and words have we felt it necessary to excuse—often without much conviction? We should consider carefully what was wrong in each case.

Then let us go through the day again. Almost certainly other people have been annoyed with us or resentful of things we have said or done to them. It is just possible that we were in the right and they were wrong to be angry or sulky. But usually we are far too ready to give ourselves the benefit of the doubt. Couldn't we have been kinder and less self-assertive in most of these instances?

Next we should do well to consider the ways in which we have spent our money or given ourselves pleasure: by eating, drinking, smoking, entertainment, dancing, sport and so on. There is nothing necessarily wrong about such pleasures, but have we, in all honesty, behaved as we would have expected Christ to behave in all these things?

Then let us think how we have served God today. Have we treated Him with respect and reverence, or have we let Him down, either openly or in private? Would He really give us a congratulatory 'Well done' tonight, or would He not feel that there is room for a great deal of improvement?

By the time we have thought things over on these lines, I doubt whether we shall have many illusions about ourselves as potential saints. If we should still think we are doing rather well, then we might with advantage take a look at the Ten Commandments or the Sermon on the Mount in St. Matthew's Gospel (Chapters 5, 6 and 7.) Even more revealing to most of us are 'My duty towards God' and 'My duty towards my neighbour' in the Prayer Book Catechism. Unless we are being plainly dishonest with ourselves and God, we ought to have a fairly clear picture of ourselves after that.

Even the best diagnosis, however, will not cure anything by itself. We must undoubtedly make the diagnosis, but the next stage is to consider whether we are really sorry for our shortcomings. We must not be dishonest about this, either. If we are not sorry, we had better admit the fact, and pray to God that we may learn to be sorry. It is bad enough to be a sinner without being shameless about the matter, too. Let us check over our failures once more in that case, and see how profoundly we ought to regret being the sort of person who does the things we have done.

Now let us test our sorrow a little. If we are really sorry for taking something which isn't ours, for example, we shall wish to restore it. If we have insulted someone, we shall want to apologize. Many of the things we have done wrong during the day can to some extent be rectified if we care enough to want to rectify them, and it is not much use saying that we are sorry unless we are prepared to make amends. We must make up our minds at once to make reparation or restitution wherever possible.

This brings us on the the next stage. The man who is sent to prison time after time we begin to regard as a hopeless case, and the would-be Christian who goes on offending against God's laws time and again is evidently less sincere than he should be. So when we have discovered where we are wrong, we must next resolve by God's help not to go wrong in the same way again. I say, 'by God's help' because we certainly cannot achieve this result without His help. At the same time, that does not relieve us of the responsibility for making every effort (and intelligent effort at that!) to avoid a repetition of our wrongdoings.

It is important to recognize in this respect that we are more likely to avoid sin if we avoid the circumstances which encourage it. If we are given to making unfriendly remarks about our neighbours, we shall best avoid the temptation to do so by keeping away from those of our acquaintance who most relish the savour of scandal. No doubt we enjoy their company, but the temptation to gossip becomes immensely stronger in such a circle. Whatever sin we are trying to break ourselves of, the less we allow ourselves the pleasure of being tempted to commit it, the more likely we are to succeed in overcoming it.

It may seem fairly obvious, but we very easily overlook the fact that nobody sins in order to be wicked, purely and simply. We sin because we like the results, or used to like them and cannot now break the habit. Overcoming temptation always means foregoing some sort of advantage, and although it is in the long run a purely illusory gain, it is filled with attraction at the moment.

There is one final step required to complete the act of penitence which we ought daily to make in our prayers, which is to give God thanks for His forgiveness. Actually, He has forgiven us long before we are prepared to ack-knowledge our guilt at all, but it is only when we have re-established a right relationship with God by making it clear that we are truly sorry that we are able properly to understand this.

We all know the relief of being friends again with someone we like or love and have fallen out with. We may not always feel this sense of relief very strongly, but this is in fact the state of affairs we should reach in our prayers when we have made a sincere act of penitence. Give thanks to God for it, and remember that His for-giveness is not something gratuitous. If it has cost us a good deal of heart-searching to ask for it, it has cost Him the life of His Son our Lord to be able to give it.

It may be helpful to summarize the four stages involved in penitence. They are:

> Self-examination
> Sorrow for sin (*i.e.* Contrition)
> Purpose to amend, and to make restitution when this is possible
> Thanksgiving to God for His forgiveness.

We cannot properly omit any of the four stages.

One pitfall we must be constantly wary of is the danger of becoming depressed and discouraged by the fact that, however penitent we are, we seem for ever to be falling into the same sins again and again. Such discouragement is itself sinful. It is a lack of trust in God. Scupoli, in his most valuable book, 'The Spiritual Combat,' has this passage:

'I suppose that you have fallen not occasionally but a hundred times in a day, not through neglect but entirely consciously. Having asked His pardon and humbled yourself the hundredth time as the first, lose no time in returning to God, to yourself and to your ordinary occupations and exercises, with the same confidence as if you had not fallen. Imitate in this matter the wise conduct of a traveller who is as brave in mind as he is feeble in body; if he happens to fall, he arises immediately and continues his journey without wasting time in useless lamentation. If after a few steps he falls again, his one thought is to rise once more and bravely pursue his journey. Thus, despite trials and disasters, he at least finishes his journey, though later than those who have fallen only seldom if at all.'

We have to remember that to be a saint—that is, an intimate friend of Almighty God—is the reward of a life-time of loving submission to Him; and we have no right to expect that He will give us such a reward merely because we are sorry. The saints themselves were often thoroughly vile people at first, but they admitted the fact and trusted that God would put them right. They were prepared to make a fresh start over and over again.

Most of *us* simply hate to be made aware of our limitations, and when we go wrong we decide to aim lower next time to avoid getting hurt. The saints have been sufficiently humble not to expect any good from themselves anyway, and instead of being discouraged they have been thankful for God's forgiveness and for a cause for fresh confidence. God can use for our ultimate good even the consequences of our own sinfulness. Thomas à Kempis, in his book *The Imitation of Christ*, imagines God talking to us like this:

'Do not think that you are entirely forsaken, although I

may have sent some trouble upon you, or may have withdraw some consolation, for so it happens to those who are travelling towards the Kingdom of Heaven. And without doubt it is more expedient for you to be tried in various ways than to have everything your own way. I know your secret thoughts, and that it is very conducive to your salvation that you should sometimes suffer, lest perhaps you should be puffed up by prosperity, and flatter yourself that you are what you are not. What I have given, I can take away; and restore again as it pleases Me. Do not assume an injured tone or lose heart; because I am quickly able to raise you up again, and to turn all your heaviness into joy. Yes, account it a special reason for rejoicing that I afflict you with sorrows and do not spare you.'

We who are so heavily indebted to God through our wilful prodigality with the credit He allows us have, nevertheless, one incalculably valuable asset. God places it at your disposal through His holy Church. It is the sacrament of Penance. There are two things we need when things go wrong: the chance to unburden ourselves to someone, and the assurance that the damage isn't permanent. God gives us both through His priest if we make our confession to him.

Obviously if you are a self-critical person—and we are pretty poor Christians unless we are self-critical—then you are bound to be perturbed by your failures, and correspondingly ashamed of them. You wish with all your heart that you could get rid of them, and you hope against hope that your shortcomings are not obvious to all the world. At the same time, it is a very lonely thing to know things about yourself which you dare not tell anyone; and it is dreadfully limiting. There seems to be no-one whose advice you can ask and whose help you can enlist.

But of course, there is! The priest who hears your confession meets precisely all those almost impossible demands we make when we need reassurance. We can tell him anything, anything whatever, because we know he cannot for any reason in heaven or earth ever disclose what he has been told in the confessional. Indeed it is part of his vocation not so much as to remember what he has been told once he has given absolution, and certainly no priest will allow his personal relationship with anyone to be affected by what they may have had to confess.

But what the penitent really wants above all is to know that 'things are going to be all right,' and it is for that very purpose that the sacrament of penance exists. Our Lord left to His church the power and authority which was needed for it to be able to say with absolute certainty that God has forgiven, and that whatever happens now is firmly in His hands. However serious or however trivial our misdeeds may be, once God has put it right, nothing else greatly matters. He may allow us still to be punished in this world for the wrongs we have done, and He will not usually suspend the logical consequences of our actions. What He *will* do is to ensure that our punishment and the very results of our sinfulness are all made to serve His purpose and further our own spiritual development, provided that we continue to put our whole trust in Him.

It is not, of course, just an assurance on general principles that we receive. That would often not be very helpful, because there is always the lurking doubt in our mind that we might be the exceptional case, that we have done the unforgiveable. No; we are given a definite absolution, personal to ourselves, assuring us of God's forgiveness for our particular case. Our Lord said to His Apostles, 'Whosoever sins ye forgive, they are forgiven unto them; whosoever sins ye retain, they are retained,'

and that same authority has been handed down from one
bishop to another and from each bishop to the priests he
has ordained, from the earliest times until now. Those
very words were a part of the form of the ordination of your
own vicar or rector or curate, and as he gives absolution
to a penitent he recalls the source of his authority : 'by
His (Christ's) authority committed to me, I absolve thee
from all thy sins in the name of the Father and of the
Son and of the Holy Ghost.' The words are, of course,
those of the Book of Common Prayer, and it is both the
right and the inexpressible privilege of any son or daughter
of the Church of England to hear those words pronounced
to them, and to know that 'Everything is going to be all
right.'

No Anglican is obliged to make a private confession to
a priest; but it is a rarity to find one who would not be
the better for doing so. Worry and 'nerves' are the
prevalent disorders of the present day, and both result
from the pressure of worldly events upon a personality
incompletely surrendered to God's purpose. Both are, at
root, evil because they stem from a lack of trust in God.
We cannot honestly claim that we are doing all we can
to get rid of them if we neglect the sacrament of penance.
We have, as the Book of Common Prayer expresses it,
failed to quieten our own conscience, and ought to open
our grief to our priest so that we may receive his absolution and serve God in peace and sincerity of heart.

It is not the business of this book to give detailed
instruction in the sacraments: there are many books
available on the subject, and any priest who normally
expects to hear confessions will gladly advise. What is
essential is that we shall realize that in our sinfulness we
have no hope but through God, and yet no need for any
other hope. With all our failures we can come to no-one

but Christ, whether directly or through His priest. The sooner we do it, the better.

5

MENTAL PRAYER

In a sense, all prayer can be summed up in the one sentence, 'Thy will be done.' The aspects of prayer which we have been considering, petition, intercession and penitence, can all be regarded from one standpoint as part of our training in knowing and doing God's will. But there is another, less widely used, method of prayer which will carry us still further along the road in the same direction. It is known as 'Discursive Meditation' or, more simply, as 'Mental Prayer.' The name is not intended to imply that the kinds of prayer we have looked at do not involve mental activity, but that in this way of praying we dispense even more completely with set forms of words and rely more upon our own minds.

Despite the somewhat forbidding name, there is nothing either profound or difficult about it. It is simply a way of thinking about the truths of the Christian faith so that they will mean more to us, both in our prayers and in our daily lives. It is not a way of prayer for everyone to use all the time. The complete beginner may well find it too difficult, and the really advanced will hardly need it, but the vast majority cannot afford to neglect it, and almost certainly the fact that you are taking the trouble to read this book is an indication that it is a way of prayer which will be profitable to you personally.

The simplest form of meditation has three main stages, the same stages we go through in thinking about almost anything. First of all, we *look and see* to find out the facts. Then we consider in what ways the facts are relevant *to us* in the actual situation we are in. Finally we decide what we have to *do* in consequence.

Suppose you are going to cross the road. You stand on the edge of the kerb and look carefully both ways before you do anything else. You *look and see,* in fact. Then you weigh up very quickly in your mind what you have seen. That car is nearly a quarter of a mile away, and the bus just coming from the opposite direction appears to be stopping. I cannot move quite as quickly as I sometimes do, because I have a heavy parcel under my arm, but I think I could get across now if I hurry.

In other words, you think, '*What does this mean to me?*' And then, almost at once, you decide *what you are going to do about it.* I'm going to cross right away, or, perhaps, I'll just wait for the car to come past first before I do.

So this three-stage pattern recurs in almost every purposeful thought-process; and it may be remarked that thought without purpose is of no use to anyone. Shakespeare's Hamlet is the classic example of a man who thought out everything beautifully, and perished because events overtook him before he had made up his mind to act.

Sometimes, of course, as in the case of crossing the road, you make up your mind so swiftly that all three stages are over in a second. Sometimes the three stages will take weeks to complete—if, for example, you are considering a step which will affect your whole future. But the process of thinking is identical, whether it takes months or seconds.

Now in meditation or mental prayer the process is exactly the same. The only real difficulty is that the material is rather unfamiliar, and constant practice will be needed to overcome this.

As a preliminary we must choose a suitable subject. Writers on prayer all recommend an incident from the life of our Lord as the best starting point. Unless you

D

know the Bible pretty well, you will find it easiest to look
for what you want in St. Mark's Gospel. The way it is
written, almost as a series of anecdotes for the most part,
makes it particularly handy for this purpose. If you follow
a scheme of daily Bible reading, so much the better.
You can then, as a rule, use your daily reading as the
theme for your meditation. You will probably find it a
help to have your Bible open in front of you during your
meditation, too.

Now, in your prayers, start by asking the help of God's
Holy Spirit in what you are going to do. Then begin right
away on the three stages which are really so very familiar
to us. First, look and see. Use your imagination to make
the incident from our Lord's life which you have chosen
as vivid as possible.

Suppose you are considering the occasion when our
Lord called His first Apostles, Peter, Andrew, James and
John. It was by the sea-side that He found them. Imagine for yourself the scene beside the Lake of Galilee:
the blue of the water lapping the shore, the arid rocks of
the hills round about, the sharp outline of shadows on
the torrid sand of the beach. Do more than merely see
it: feel it, smell it, as if you were a part of it. Taste the
salt tang in the air, hear the distant shouts of the fisher-
folk, the grate of a boat's keel on the sand, feel the heat
of the sun on the crown of your head. You are there
yourself; or better still, the sea of Galilee is here, with
you, in your own room.

Here is Jesus, walking at the water's edge towards the
boats. You can see His face, hear His voice, watch His
gestures. Notice the expression on His features. See the
reaction of the fishermen to His uncompromising demand,
'Follow me'—incredulity, surprise, hesitation and then a
recognition of His authority and a decision to obey

whatever the cost.

Look and see. Look until you know every detail of the scene. See precisely what happens, in all its significance.

Here is what St. François de Sales says about this part of a meditation in his *Introduction to the Devout Life:*

'This is what some call the 'composition of place,' others the 'interior lesson.' It is nothing other than bringing before one's imagination the matter of the incident which one wishes to consider, as if it were really and actually taking place in one's own presence—for example, if you wish to meditate upon our Lord as the gospel writers describe Him. By means of this imagining we shut up our mind within the incident we wish to meditate upon, so that it shall not go running here and there, any more than a bird which we shut up in a cage.'

Now move on in your thought, without letting go of what you can already see. Think, 'What does this mean to me?' You have seen what the disciples saw all those centuries ago, and you have seen how it affected them. Our Lord's demands on you are no less urgent, no less uncompromising, no less absolute.

Here, of course, is where your meditation becomes entirely a personal business. The question is not, 'What does this mean for Tom, Dick and Harry, or for the Archbishop of Canterbury or for John Brown the butcher's boy?' but 'What does this mean for *you*, you personally and no-one else?'

What might it mean? It certainly means this: that Christ is making a total demand upon you, just as He was upon His first Apostles. They had to give up their old way of life completely and start afresh, and we must expect to be totally committed to God's purpose, too. Beyond that, it is your own business to find out what this involves in your own circumstances.

The third stage of this method of praying is also a personal matter. 'What are you going to do about it?' In this, one must be very, very chary of far-reaching decisions which would materially change one's way of life. The purpose of prayer is not to cause upheavals, but to bring us into a closer relationship with God; and the resolution simply to do our best to 'keep close to God' for the rest of the day may well be the most effective of all resolutions. It is ourselves we have to change, not our circumstances, and this is inevitably a long, slow process. It calls for patience, not dramatic gestures, and the most practical resolutions are those with strictly limited objectives—to avoid brusqueness with your wife or niggardliness over your prayer-time or unnecessary curiosity about other people's affairs, for instance.

Finish your meditation by asking the help of God's Holy Spirit in keeping your resolution, just for today. The simpler your prayer, the better it will be, and the same applies to your resolution.

Mental prayer, then, is not a very difficult form of prayer, although it does require a certain amount of patience and effort. Daily practice is essential and a useful meditation will take at least ten minutes or a quarter of an hour of quiet concentration. The material must be well chewed over to extract all the goodness from it, and one can scarcely do this in less time, even having read the subject-matter over beforehand.

As we become accustomed to the method, we shall find it profitable to develop what the classical teachers of mental prayer call 'colloquies': that is to say, we imagine ourselves actually in conversation with our Lord in the scene we have before us. If He is vividly present to us, we can bring to Him in imagination our problems and difficulties, we can thank Him for His favours to us, we can tell Him of our sorrow for causing Him displeasure. The words we put into His mouth will, of course, be words essentially of our own choosing, but the more vividly we have pictured Him, the more clearly we shall know what He might truly say to us. Those words of His which are recorded in the Gospels will often spring to our minds as words He might well speak to us in our own circumstances.

To many people it will be helpful to picture our Lord in the so-called 'hidden years' before His public ministry, when His daily task was to labour at the carpenter's bench, to deal with village customers, to attend to His family affairs. He had to face just those very situations which arise in *our* lives, and He was able always to find a way in perfect accord with the will of His Father.

When we have acquired the habit of meditation, we can take almost any aspect of the Christian faith as our subject matter. It need not be an incident at all. To meditate upon the love of God or the doctrine of the Holy Trinity brings one very near to the heart of the matter. But that kind of topic is rather too ambitious at the outset.

It should be self-evident that profitable meditation depends upon sound knowledge, and to make any real progress we need a scheme of reading quite apart from the basic minimum of bible reading. We should aim at spending at least ten minutes in the day reading a book on prayer or the spiritual life. To quote St. John of the Cross, perhaps the greatest of all writers on prayer:

'It is indeed necessary for the soul to be given material for meditation, and to make interior acts on its own account, to take advantage of the spiritual heat and fire which comes from the senses. This is necessary in order to accustom the senses and desires to good things, so that, being fed with this delight, they may become detached from the world.'

The choice of one's spiritual reading is of great importance. The great classic is Thomas à Kempis' *The Imitation of Christ*, easily obtainable from almost any large bookshop in any one of a dozen different editions. There is no-one who will not profit from reading it; but it must be read *prayerfully*. One cannot read it like a novel, with the radio switched on or a buzz of conversation in the room. Nor must you expect to get through it quickly, or its savour will be lost. The best way to use such a book is to read no more than a page or even half a page at a time. Pause at each sentence to think over what you have just read, and to consider what it means to you. Your reading will, in fact, be like a series of short meditations, a method which will itself help you to acquire the art of meditation. Père de Caussade gives this advice:

'Spend more time in nourishing your soul with good spiritual reading. To make this nourishment the more beneficial, let this be your method of taking it. Begin by entering the presence of God and by begging His help. Read gently and slowly, a word at a time, so that you may interpret your subject with your soul rather than with your intelligence. At the end of each paragraph pause for as long as it would take you to say the Lord's Prayer, or even for a little longer, to appreciate what you have read. When you notice that your attention is wandering, go back to your reading, constantly making similar pauses. If you find the above method useful, there is nothing to prevent your adopting it during the time set aside for meditation.'

Of course, meditation must never become the be all and end all of our prayer. Far from it. The more we learn about the life of prayer, the more we see how wide is its scope, and the more we see which we have still to learn.

Meditation in particular should lead us on quite gradually to more profound and sincere and prolonged praise and adoration. After a few more years we may hope to be ready for a still more advanced way of prayer.

You may feel already that to follow all the suggestions made in these pages will take up a great deal of your time. So it will. What is more, that part of your day which is not spent in conscious prayer will be spent rather differently if your prayers are sincere. Prayer is *meant* to affect your daily life, and if it does not, it is failing dismally. We must be prepared for our prayers to make havoc of our way of life, or we shall never learn to pray at all.

Meanwhile, spiritual reading not only helps us by letting us see the great spiritual masters at prayer: it both makes clearer the purpose of prayer, and shows us how it finds its direct application in everyday life. Above all, spiritual reading will help to do what our prayers and all our meditation should be doing: it will give us a deeper knowledge of God's infinite love for us, and it will strengthen *our* love for Him. As we come to love God more, we shall be the more eager to do His will, and the more capable of recognizing it in every circumstance we meet.

6

THE OBJECT IN HAND

WE shall not have been praying very long before we begin to strike against a snag which to a greater or less degree affects the prayers of everyone, sinner and saint alike: the problem of how to keep our mind on the job in hand.

When we ought to be praying, we find our attention wandering to every sort of mundane affair, in an altogether disconcerting fashion. We mean to concentrate, but each new idea brings associations which lead us back into a world of trivialities. We thank God for our health and wonder when we shall find time to get a new bottle of aspirins from the chemist. Intercession for the church-warden who happens to be a butcher leads to a sudden feeling that we forgot to order the pork chops for tomorrow's dinner party, and the whole meal has been re-planned and checked over in our mind before the realization comes that this is not prayer. Now we have only five minutes left of our prayer-time before the garden claims our urgent attention. The herbaceous border must be weeded before it starts raining again, and—there we are again with another quite different digression which is wasting still more time.

'Perhaps,' we think to ourselves, 'I might do better tomorrow. This session is going so badly I wish it were over!' Bad prayers so soon become boring prayers. It must be wonderful to be a saintly person and to kneel, wrapped up in prayer, calmly, serenely, timelessly!

But let us take a close-up view of a saint. It is quite surprising. Says St. Teresa of Avila, one of the greatest of all authorities on prayer, 'Very often, over a period of several years, I was more occupied in wishing my hour of prayer were over, and in listening whenever the clock struck, than in thinking of things that were good.'

If so great a saint as Teresa was not proof against the wandering of her attention during her prayers, it is not to be wondered at that we do not succeed where she failed. At the same time, there are ways and means of minimising its effect, and perhaps in the end of over-coming the difficulty altogether as she did.

The first principle is to pay as little attention to dis-tractions as we possibly can. We must not be impatient with ourselves for being scatter-brained. Far better to be simply mildly amused by the ridiculousness of the situation: we are so feeble-minded that even the presence of Almighty God does not sufficiently impress us to keep our interest!

When we find that our attention has wandered, we must quite gently return to the prayer we were making, and cease to concern ourselves with the distracting thought. It is not a necessary thought, because nothing is necessary in our prayer-time but to attend to God. It cannot be as important as our prayer, and if it is an important thought at all it will certainly return at a more convenient time.

What we cannot do is to decide *not* to think about a particular matter. Mark Twain made the point rather neatly when he challenged a friend to spend two minutes *not* thinking at all of the word 'Hippopotamus.' The effort itself guarantees failure. We need a positive line of thought which will leave no room for anything else in our mind.

The second principle is to face God squarely all the time we are praying. Don't, as it were, offer God a profile view of yourself, or think of Him as if He were a pronoun in the third person. See Him full-face. Address yourself directly to Him, and remember that you have *His* concentrated attention. We need to use our imagination to remember His divine presence, but that Presence is entirely real. It is Itself no figment of the imagination.

What we must never do is to worry that we have wasted our time in prayer by letting our attention wander. Thoughts which refuse to be silenced can very often be actually woven into the fabric of our prayer, and made the subject of a phase of that prayer. It is much better to treat them as material for prayer than to attempt violently to rid ourselves of them. The very effort gives them an importance they do not merit, and fatally disturbs our own peace of mind into the bargain.

I recall once during the war watching a company of infantrymen trying to haul a heavily laden raft across a river in spate along a rope moored to the two banks. The swollen torrent threatened at any moment to overturn the ill-balanced craft, and fifty or sixty men sweated and strained on a bafflingly complicated system of ropes intended to maintain some sort of equilibrium and to haul the load through the swirling flood.

Half an hour later a section of Royal Engineers had the same problem to face. They put a rope across the river, moored it to the further bank and attached their raft to the other end. Without further ado they cast the raft adrift, and with a single sapper holding a guide rope on the bank, they stood and watched the powerful stream gently swing the raft, pendulum-wise, to the other side.

The lesson should not be wasted on anyone who wishes to make progress in the spiritual life. When the current of our own waywardness, or indeed of the world as a whole, is irresistible, there is always a way in which we can use that energy. To strive against the flood is to invite frustration and often sheer failure. Remember that God is always in control of all things, and that any fierce struggling must inevitably be a struggling against God Himself. To accept our distractions in prayer for God's sake is quite the most effective way of bringing our mind back into His orbit, and the choice of Him in preference to the distracting thought is itself a most acceptable prayer.

At the same time, we cannot expect our mind to be concentrated and undistracted in our prayers if we constantly allow it to run unfettered where it will in the remaining hours of the day. The same method of quietly laying aside useless thoughts is as necessary when we are riding on a bus or washing up after breakfast as it is in our meditation: mental discipline is not an umbrella which we can put up or down at will.

To many people it comes as a shock to realize just how little good comes of most of that mental activity which fills our idle moments. Our minds are continually in movement throughout our waking hours, yet mostly engaged in thoughts which do us more harm than good. To worry about the past which we cannot change or about the future which is in God's hands is a fruitless occupation.

To comb wearily over our tangled recollection of a conversation, wondering whether we made fools of ourselves, is a quite useless dissipation of energy. To hope to devise a fool-proof formula for conducting the next conversation is equally futile. We must accept ourselves as we are, and if we have the sense to admit to God that we *are* fools, then we may learn to face with equanimity the prospect of other people finding it out for themselves. By the same token, it is pointless for us to confess to God that we are miserable sinners and then to hope that nobody else will notice the fact. Nor can we allow ourselves the luxury of mentally chewing over our neighbour's shortcomings if we mean to learn to love him.

Once more, let it be stressed that we cannot simply banish such thoughts from our minds. They must either be taken into a prayer—yes, even on the bus or in the kitchen—or they must be replaced by something more positive. To use short 'ejaculations' or 'aspirations' during the day is the most obvious way of supplying our mind with alternative material. A phrase such as, 'Lord, have mercy,' 'Jesus, be with me,' or 'Lord, bless, preserve and keep us' will rapidly bring our mind back to a state of recollection—recollection of the ubiquitous and continual presence of God, and of His care and providence for all men. That awareness of the presence of God which we practise on our knees must 'spread over' into every other activity of our day.

St. François de Sales offers the simple but thoroughly practical suggestion that we ought never to leave our prayers without picking for ourselves a 'spiritual bouquet' which we may carry with us throughout the day to re-mind us of the garden of prayer in which we have walked with God. One single thought which will recall to us the prayer we made will often sweeten the rest of the day. What is more, it will tend to ensure that our prayers do not become detached from our daily life, and so lose that attachment to reality which is both their safeguard and their final purpose.

There is still perhaps still one further warning to be given. We must beware of hedging our prayers about with so many formal defences against distraction that we shut out the possibility of making contact with God at

all. We ought never to plan our prayers so rigidly that
we feel we must at all costs get through a given programme
in a given time. Such inflexibility will inevitably lead to
an exclusion of any action by the Holy Spirit. As we have
seen, He suggests so very gently what He wishes of us
that any firmness on our part will easily shout Him down.
We do well to come to our prayers with some sort of a
plan, but wherever we find a point at which we are in-
clined to linger, there we should be content to rest until
another point attracts our attention.

So long as we remain reverently in the presence of God,
it matters very little what we do in His presence. He will
see to it that our time is not wasted. When prayer is most
truly prayer, it is not something we do for God, but
something which God in His infinite tenderness does for
us. Our own personal satisfaction with our prayers
matters not a scrap.

Nevertheless, despite all that has been said, it remains
true that the most disciplined mind finds it difficult to
give altogether undistracted attention to God when the
day's work looms ahead or when, in the evening, a clatter
of worldly problems still echoes in the background. The
example of our Lord, of His disciples, of the great men of
prayer in the Old Testament and of Christian saints in
more recent times is unanimous here. It is an example of
quiet withdrawal from all affairs for some days at a
stretch, so that a rested and quiet mind may give its whole
attention to God.

It may at first sight appear somewhat impracticable for
us to follow their example in present day circumstances.
Yet in fact there exist all over the country 'retreat houses'
where one may spend just such a period of spiritual
recreation, and to which men and women and young
people from every walk of life come annually in their

thousands. A long-week-end, better still four or five days, is not difficult to find if one is convinced of the value of such a respite, and an annual 'retreat' along these lines is of incalculable value to one who cares for the things of God.

Almost always it is possible to go into retreat with ten or twenty other people, who will join together in the chapel of the retreat house for prayers three or four times in the course of each day, spending the remaining time quietly on their own. An experienced priest will be with them as 'retreat conductor.' His part is to give one or two short addresses each day to guide the retreatants in their devotions, and to be at hand to give private help and advice to any who wish it.

In the traditional retreat complete silence is kept at all times outside chapel services, so that one has not even the responsibility of social intercourse with one's fellow retreatants. Indeed, the first impression most people have of being in retreat is one of blessed and unparalleled release from the responsibilities of their everyday life. So long as the retreat lasts, nothing and no-one can make demands except God, and the rest of the world may go its own way.

In the silence and tranquillity of such a time, one's own standard of values becomes re-adjusted to those values which have eternal significance. One can view one's own way of life with a degree of disinterestedness and detachment which is otherwise seldom possible.

One can re-assess the role for which God has cast us, and learn anew from Him the principles which underlie His purpose for us. It is no more a time of idleness than the time which your car spends in the garage workshop undergoing maintenance is a time of idleness. Rather it is that essential phase in the existence of any mechanism, human or otherwise, in which it is restored to its optimum condition ready for the next period of activity.

The effect of a good retreat upon our prayers for months afterwards has to be experienced to be understood. It provides, so to speak, a norm of reality against which the distractions and vicissitudes of our daily prayers can be seen in their true perspective. It helps us to recognize our feelings, religious or emotional, as the transient whims they really are, and to recall that our true life is immeasurably more soundly based, firm rooted upon the Rock which is Christ.

7

FEELINGS, GUIDANCE AND DIRECTION

MODERN cynicism seldom tires of pointing out to us one of the great dangers of prayer, that we may very easily mistake the dictates of our own sub-conscious mind for an expression of the will of God. The danger is undoubtedly a very real one, but it was not left to modern psychology to discover the fact. The great spiritual masters of all ages have been fully aware of it, and the Christian who pays heed to their advice need have no serious fears on this score.

The strongest weapon in our armoury against this danger is a recognition of the fact that our feelings are quite the least reliable part of our human make-up. To those brought up in certain traditions of Christianity, this may at first appear rather startling. We all delight in praying when we *feel* that God is with us, just as we enjoy our worship most when we *feel* carried away by it. Some people even go so far as to say that they *must feel* that they are praying if their prayers are to be sincere. A moment's consideration will show how dangerous such a belief can be. May I illustrate the danger?

I vividly recall one Monday morning passing a friend in the street. 'How are you this morning?' I inquired, knowing that he had not been well.

'I feel absolutely first rate! I was saying to my wife a few minutes ago that I haven't been on form for months, and it's wonderful to feel fit again,' he replied.

That evening my friend underwent an operation for a perforated appendix, and was in hospital for weeks!

I do not doubt for a moment that my friend really did

feel wonderfully well when he spoke to me, but inside him was a centre of disease which but for recent advances in surgery would almost certainly have been fatal. I do not claim, of course, that our feelings are always so greatly in error, but I would stress that they *can* be, and are more often than we suspect, extremely unreliable. They are a part of the animal nature we considered in an earlier chapter, and a wise person uses the more typically human capacity of rational thinking to guide him in his decision and opinions. When God allows us to feel devout we can be glad of it. When He lets us feel His presence we ought to enjoy the delight of it. But when He doesn't do either, we must rely on what we know to be true, His promise that, 'I am with you alway, even unto the end of the world,' and ignore our feelings or the lack of them.

There is no phase of our prayers at which this is more important than when we come to God to ask for the guidance of His Holy Spirit in a particular matter. The danger that the guidance we receive may be that of our own feelings—our sub-conscious mind, if you prefer the term—is at its greatest at this point. We intentionally try not to let our own judgment obtrude, and we often do succeed in stopping up the channels of our conscious thought. The result is, as modern psychologists have demonstrated, that our sub-conscious mind very readily takes control; and our sub-conscious mind can be quite unscrupulous in its libidinous egocentricity. The tragedy is that we are easily persuaded under such circumstances that we have been given a direct revelation by God as to what we ought to do, and therefore to act upon the suggestion with inflexible purpose. The most irrational impulse of self-interest is being treated as if it were the purest expression of the will of God.

Perhaps it is because we are so familiar with instances

E

in Holy Scripture in which God has given His guidance by directly addressing His servants that we expect to be similarly favoured. There are unquestionably instances in the lives of the saints when, even in comparatively recent times, God has spoken plainly to them. Nevertheless, it must be appreciated that such cases are rare to a degree. There may be one or two conclusive instances in a generation, but we can take it for granted, as St. John of the Cross points out, that God will not go outside the normal channels of grace to direct our comparatively trivial concerns.

What, then, is the normal channel of divine guidance? Augustine Baker, a great seventeenth century authority on the spiritual life, is the classical English writer on the subject. He explains that, in the vast majority of cases, our own reasoned judgment acting in the light of the teaching of the Bible and Church as to what is right and wrong must be expected to provide the answer to our perplexities. The more we endeavour to put into practice what we know of the will of God in each and every circumstance, the more experience we shall have of what is involved in doing God's will, and the sounder will be our decision.

When we need guidance in a particularly critical matter, we ought rather to apply our knowledge of this established channel than to entrust ourselves to an unknown and hazardous method of determining God's purpose. And so, says Augustine Baker,

'In seeking to know the divine will by prayer, let not the person make the subject and business of his recollection be the framing of a direct prayer about the matter. Neither let him in his prayer entertain any discoursing, debating thoughts in his imagination or understanding about it..... because by such proceedings our prayers will be turned into a distracting meditation; because by so doing we incur the danger of mistaking our own imagination or natural inclination for the divine light; because such discoursing in time of prayer is anything else but prayer.

'Let not the soul, therefore, that is desirous by prayer to obtain light from God in a doubtful matter alter anything in the order and manner of her accustomed recollections. Let her be sure to take great care not to give way to any hope or desire that God should reconcile His will unto her by any extraordinary way, as by ministry of angels, strange revelations, voices, etc.'

Divine guidance will, in fact, come primarily through our own intention to submit to God's will, so that our own hopes and fears, ambitions and anxieties do not lead us to a wrong decision. With a mind quietened by this intention and by the presence of God's Holy Spirit, we shall be able, *outside our prayer time*, to view the problem unhindered and unswayed by our natural prejudices and turbulence of mind. It will also be possible for God to show us, very, very gently, that the factors are not necessarily such as we saw them to begin with.

In the end, the decision will always be left to us, because God will not take away our free will however much we ask Him to do so. But the more closely we conform in everything to God's will, the more easily we shall discover His will in any particular circumstance. It is no mere quibble to add that we not infrequently find in the end that we have, as we say, 'No choice in the matter.' God's will is paramount everywhere at all times, and what is impossible cannot ever be in accordance with His will. When we really have 'no choice,' it is the clearest proof of all that what we have to do is that which God wills us to do, and we should give ourselves no more concern about it. If our feelings are still uneasy, that is because they are misguided, and the more assiduously we ignore them, the more quickly they will subside and allow us to get on with the job peaceably.

Unfortunately it is not only at times of crisis that our feelings are apt to have a harmful effect upon our prayers. There are for all of us who try to pray with any regularity times when we feel appallingly discouraged, and in particular become convinced that God has either deserted us or flatly opposes our efforts to do His will.

The more technical books refer to such states as 'aridity' and 'desolation.' Sooner or later they occur to all of us, sometimes for brief periods, sometimes for months or even years on end. Often they recur after a period during which we have seemed to recover a more satisfying equilibrium in our prayers, and always such phases are to a greater or less extent the source of real distress. We may suffer in silence for a time, but in the end we tend either to complain bitterly against God or else to give up hope altogether—and also our habits of prayer.

Quite the most effective defence against such discouragement is the realization that it is a thoroughly normal state in those who pray, and that it is certainly to be regarded as an intentional part of God's plan for training us in prayer. At such a time we must on no account give up our prayers, nor make a radical alteration in the pattern of them in an effort to improve matters. We must at all costs carry on so far as possible as if nothing had happened; and we shall find quite certainly that the phase will pass.

When we consider the matter, of course, we realize that so long as our prayers are pleasant and seem to bring the intense delight of real contact with God, all our natural inclinations lead us to continue them. It requires no great amount of virtue to do so. But when our prayers bring us nothing but discomfort and we continue them simply in the conviction that God wants us to do so, evidently the prayers are more pleasing to God just because they are less pleasing to ourselves. We are doing something for God without apparently receiving anything in return, which is a sign of real love for Him even though we may not feel it. A man shows considerably more love for his wife when he rolls the front lawn for her, which he hates doing, than when he takes her to the theatre to see a play they both enjoy!

We need to hold firmly to the truth that God never does anything which will not be for our ultimate good, and when He makes even our very prayers uncomfortable, it is a sign that He places a great deal of confidence in us. He trusts us to trust Him, even when He is hurting us. If He never made our prayers anything but a pleasure, there would be real truth in the cynic's contention that prayer is a form of escapism from the hard realities of life. God, of His infinite goodness, brings those realities into the very heart of our prayer-life so that we may learn the truth that religion is not a cosy refuge for the weaklings of this world, but is an exercise demanding the highest moral courage. Heroes are not made on feather beds!

When this dryness occurs in our prayers, and there seems to be a barren desert where once we enjoyed the lush beauties of a summer garden, we should so far as we can thank God for it, and then pay as little attention to it as possible. It is essential to stand by our established habits of prayer. Habits are made to keep us going in times like these, and our spiritual stamina will be immensely strengthened for having seen us through such a period.

When it is over, we shall not infrequently see the gain we have made, and understand that it has been worth the struggle. If we do not see the gain, it will be none the less real for that.

Of course, although one can get a great deal of help at such times from books on the spiritual life, and still more from the Bible, it is inevitably a lonely and disheartening business. For most people there is enormous benefit in having someone to talk to about these matters, especially someone who is well versed in the life of prayer. The Caroline bishop, Jeremy Taylor, writes in his most valuable book *Holy Living* :

'To the same purpose it is of great use that he who would preserve his humility should choose some spiritual person to whom he shall oblige himself to discover his very thoughts and fancies, every act of his and all his intercourse with others in which there may be danger; that by such openness of spirit he may expose every blast of vain-glory; every idle thought to be chastened and lessened by the rod of spiritual discipline; and he that shall find himself tied to confess every proud thought, every vanity of his spirit, will also perceive they must not dwell with him, nor find any kindness from him.

'The humble man trusts not to his own discretion, but in matters of concernment relies rather upon the judgment of his friends, counsellors or spiritual guides.'

Such a person, who will guide us through the pitfalls of Christian living and praying, we call nowadays a Spiritual Director, and normally we should choose as a director a priest who is particularly qualified by his studies to advise on spiritual matters.

Not least among the advantages of having such a guide is the fact that if we will put ourselves into his hands in spiritual matters, he can relieve us of the very serious burden of always being the judge in our own cause. The more progress we make, the more anxious we are apt to become as to whether we are really doing God's will in any particular instance, or whether we are giving ourselves an unwarranted benefit of the doubt.

The discipline of deferring to someone else's judgment is not always a congenial one, but the alternative is to make ourselves always the final arbiter of our own actions. Our case would be rather like that of a patient who expects both to diagnose his own ailment and to prescribe all his own medicine on the grounds that he knows himself better than any doctor. Indeed in the case of spiritual difficulties it is rather more serious, for the determined self-reliance which such an attitude entails is itself a serious spiritual ill. It cuts at the very root of that humility which is essential in any who would approach the throne of God.

It is perhaps for this reason that we most need the help of a spiritual director. We are too much with ourselves, too close up to the picture as it were, to see clearly the perspective. Our emotions are too frequently and too heavily engaged for us to achieve an unbiassed judgment. The discipline of life which alone can overcome this difficulty can be safely assessed only by someone outside ourselves.

It is, after all, essential for the Christian to have a 'rule of life' if he is not to be continually at the mercy of his feelings. Actually we all *have* a 'rule of life,' whether consciously or unconsciously: we get up at such and such a time, have our meals according to a time-table or to varying circumstances, spend our money on some sort of principles however haphazard.

The Christian's rule of life ought to be a consciously formulated one, with the underlying object of relating as many of our activities as possible to the purposes of God. Apart from the need for habitual times of prayer, we ought to have some rule of public worship, of fasting, of giving money in support of the Church's work. Only a properly arranged rule will ensure that such matters are not neglected when they do not accord with our feelings.

Our rule must obviously be a personal one, for no two people live in the same circumstances. We have widely differing incomes, hours of work, family responsibilities and so on. The Church cannot in the nature of things lay down more than the very minimum obligations which should be binding upon all her children. At the same time, this minimum is not sufficient to bring us very far along the road of submission to God in all things.

In drawing up our rule, we shall do well to enlist the aid of a spiritual director who can fairly say what sort of rule we might be able to keep. His experience will be invaluable in holding the balance between an unattainable idealism and a triviality which makes no demands at all upon ourselves, our time, our energy or our money. There is obvious advantage in our director being also our confessor, for the priest who hears our confessions is able better than anyone else to judge of our spiritual potentialities.

It is, indeed, barely possible to overestimate the value to our spiritual well-being of a faithful director. He is uniquely equipped to steer us through the storms in which our feelings may so easily deflect us from the principles of sound navigation. Yet we must never lose sight of the fact that God is Himself the final court of appeal. Our main task is to get to know *Him*, and such knowledge can be achieved only by regular, frequent and prolonged contact at the most intimate level of our prayer.

8

GIVING GOD HIS DUE

EVERYTHING which has been said throughout these pages really adds up to this : we have to learn to get away from compulsive preoccupation with the world and with ourselves, and *be with God* in prayer. The more we concentrate upon God and upon His favours to us, the less we shall be misled by anything less important.

In this chapter, then, we must consider two further aspects of prayer, both closely connected to each other and of extreme importance if we are to develop any depth in our spiritual life. The two aspects are those of praise and thanksgiving.

Thanksgiving ought actually to follow on quite naturally from the prayer of petition. We ask God for what we need, both for ourselves and for other people, and it is no more than common courtesy to God to thank Him when He gives what we ask for. It is both surprising and distressing to realize how slack most people tend to be about this, then. Probably they would say that they are not so much ungrateful as unmindful or forgetful, but that seems to be a distinction without a difference.

We recognize that we ought to be grateful for favours received, whether from God or from other people. What we do not always realize is that we need actively to *train* ourselves in gratitude. Being grateful does not come naturally to us, any more than any other virtue. We teach small children to be grateful because it helps them not to be grasping or to take gifts as no more than their due. They are less likely to be greedy and selfish if they recognize that things which are given to them are the result of a generosity in others, and not something they have a right to. We teach them by making them say 'please' and 'thank-you' for everything as they receive it, but it can be a very long, hard struggle before a child will say the magic words without having to be prompted.

We, too, need to learn gratitude for just the same reasons that a child does, and we can learn it only by using the same process. We have to remind ourselves a hundred times a day to say 'thank-you' to God for everything we have and are, and in time we shall come to realize how much we have to be grateful to Him for.

One very sound idea is always to say grace before meals. It serves as a reminder that our food is God's gift to us, and is also a most valuable aid to forming the habit of gratitude. What is more, the underlying principle is one that can and should be extended to all those hundreds of occasions each day when there is something for which we might equally well say a silent, 'Thanks be to God.'

When you get out of bed on a fresh spring morning, do you say thank-you to God for it? It is His gift! Do we thank God for a good home when we go off to work, or for a steady job when we arrive at the factory or office or wherever we earn our living? Do we thank God for good health when we see an ambulance, for good sight when we pass an optician's, for a good appetite when it comes to lunch time? We have absolutely nothing which has not come from God, and whatever we are, we are what He has made us. The most 'self-made' man in the world lives only because God gives him air to breathe and the strength to inhale it: his life is in God's hand, and it is only by God's favour that he remains alive from one minute to the next.

The writers of the Old Testament thought of even so ordinary a thing as a shower of rain as a direct miracle, and in a very true sense they were right. Every shower, every beam of sunlight, comes to us through the purposeful providence of God. It is not just due to 'chance' or to blind natural laws, but it is a gift of God designed by His infinite wisdom to further His all-embracing plan. We may hate the wet weather on a Bank Holiday, but we know that it will do good somewhere, and to ourselves it can be a blessing if it teaches us to be patient and independent of the material circumstances of our lives.

It is not easy optimism on St. Paul's part when he says that all things work together for good to them that love God. Rather it is an expression of his understanding of the almost incredible and quite incomprehensible care which God shows for every one of His creatures in all His doings. The sun shines no less brightly for the criminal than for the saint. The free air is equally life-giving to both of them, and a drink of cold water is just as refreshing to each, whether they are grateful for it or not. The world of nature is meaningless to us if.it does not serve to bring to mind the one whose handiwork it is.

St. Augustine reminds of this in a very beautiful passage in his *Confessions*:

'I asked the earth,' he says, 'and it answered me, 'I am not God,' and whatsoever are in it confessed the same. I asked the sea and the deeps and the living creeping things, and they answered, 'We are not God, seek above us.' I asked the moving air; and the whole air with its inhabitants answered, 'Be not deceived, I am not He.' I asked the heavens, sun, moon, stars, 'Nor,' say they, 'are we the God whom thou seekest.' And I replied unto all the things which encompass the door of my flesh, 'Ye have told me of my God, that ye are not He; tell me something of Him.' And they cried out with a loud voice, 'He made us!' '

Once we have acquired the habit of recognizing God's action in everything and giving Him credit for it, we find that anything and everything can lead our thoughts towards God. And when we begin to see this vision of God, however dimly, we begin to enter much more fully into a still more important aspect of prayer—*praise*.

It is not easy to define praise. Praise, worship, adoration —they all mean much the same thing, and, like thanksgiving, they depend basically upon an attitude of mind. It is the same attitude of mind which we can see in a young man who is head over heels in love. He is torn between two extremes: he sees in his mind someone as remote from him as the stars, yet at the same time he longs for nothing so much as her smile of recognition, the closeness of her presence, the intimacy of her touch. He cannot find words to tell her what he feels. He can only say, 'I love you,' over and over again, and hope that it does not sound callow.

This is precisely the problem that we are faced with in trying to put into words our praise for God. But the fact that we have no adequate words for it is no reason for leaving it out of account. Time spent in trying to praise God is the most valuable part of all our prayer time. If we cannot put what we want to say into words at all, that does not matter. God will understand.

If you feel very strongly the need of words here, use the forms which the Church has used for centuries. 'Glory be to the Father, and to the Son, and to the Holy Ghost; as it was in the beginning, is now, and ever shall be, world without end; Amen.' It is an act of pure praise which you can say time and again without tiring of it. Or you might use the Tersanctus, 'Holy, holy, holy, Lord God of Hosts. Heaven and earth are full of Thy glory; glory be to Thee, O Lord most high.' They are the words which the great prophet Isaiah heard the angels repeating ceaselessly in praise of God, and we can hardly do better than to make them our own.

The Te Deum or the Gloria in Excelsis are more extended acts of praise which we might use in our prayers and a good many popular hymns fall in the same class. At the same time, it is well to bear in mind that a short phrase is often more expressive than a long sequence of clauses.

Do not be afraid of repetition in this part of your prayers, or in any other part for that matter. It is true that our Lord condemned *vain* repetition as an un-Christian thing, but He taught and practised repetition which has meaning and purpose. In His own most earnest prayer of all, in the Garden of Gethsemane before His crucifixion, He had no words but these: 'O my Father, if it be possible, let this cup pass away from me; nevertheless, not as I will, but as Thou wilt.' The Gospel narratives make it clear that He repeated the words over and over again, presumably hour on end.

Remember, too, Christ's parable of the widow who finally got satisfaction from a corrupt judge by wearing him out with her incessant request, 'Avenge me of my adversary.' That was repetition, most certainly, but it was not *vain* repetition, and our Lord pointed to it as a pattern of all Christian prayer. St. Francis of Assisi used to spend whole nights in prayer repeating continually the words, 'My God and my All.' There is no shortage of phrases which we can all use in this way; for example, 'All praise, all glory be to Thee, Lord Jesus Christ.' Or, 'We praise Thee, we bless Thee, our Father and King.' Or, 'Thy kingdom come, O Christ.' Or, 'Blessed art Thou, Lord God, and worthy to be praised and glorified and exalted above all for ever.'

The young lover never tires of saying, 'I love you,' and a woman never tires of hearing it, simply because some words are needed, and there do not seem to be any others. God, too, evidently prefers us to use the same words over and over again in praise of Him, rather than that we should cease to praise Him at all.

There is one simple device which some people find attractive if they dislike the monotony of literal repetition and wish for something to say which does not entail careful thinking out as one goes along. Simply use our Lord's name, repeated rhythmically three times over, and then add a phrase of your own making, like this: 'Jesus, Jesus, Jesus, I worship you. Jesus, Jesus, Jesus, I praise you. Jesus, Jesus, Jesus, I love you. Jesus, Jesus, Jesus, I glorify you. Jesus, Jesus, Jesus, save us. Jesus, Jesus, Jesus, have mercy upon us.' And so on, quite slowly and reverently. You can make such a prayer for a long period without any sense of boredom and with no necessity to hunt for words or ideas.

The important thing, as we have seen, is the worshipping attitude of mind. If we can hold on to that without any words at all for a time, so much the better. At all events, let us never leave our prayers without a conscious act of thanksgiving to God, and a conscious time of praise and adoration for Him. In the last analysis it is the one and only thing we can do for God. It is also our supreme opportunity to join in harmony with the immense purpose of the whole universe. If we neglect it, the very stones will cry out!

9

LIVING SACRIFICE

WHAT we must never lose sight of in our prayers is that the whole object is to learn to praise God not only with our lips but with our whole personality, in every aspect of our lives. It brings us to the logical climax of all the various modes of prayer which we have considered, what is sometimes called, 'The prayer of Self-offering.' It is the prayer in which we offer ourselves to God *unreservedly* for His purpose, to do whatever He wants us to do, to put up with whatever He calls us to put up with. Unreservedly.

We shall have to face the fact that this is going to be a painful process. We are too fond of our own way, too frightened of being hurt, for it to be anything else. That is why this kind of prayer naturally follows all the others. Unless we have begun to achieve real contact with God, we shall have no adequate incentive to make this kind of prayer with sincerity. But it *must* be made.

There is not usually much difficulty about putting this prayer into words once we are prepared to make it. There is a very lovely old prayer which puts it in a nutshell: 'Wherever, whenever and however Thy glory may best be served; there, then and in that state would I, Thy servant be.'

The most effective preparation for making such a prayer is quite simply to school oneself not so much as to consider what are one's likes and dislikes! The less attention they receive, the less they make themselves a nuisance to us. St. Paul could say that, 'I have learnt in whatsoever state I am, therewith to be content.' It requires infinitely more self-discipline than one might believe unless one has tried to achieve it, but it is the only way of making sure that we can be content to do God's will instead of following our own inclinations.

The man who dislikes what he is given for breakfast can all too easily start the day in a fit of bad temper which will drive out all the love he should have for his fellow men. The woman who is simply dying for a cup of tea can become quite oblivious of the kindness and courtesy due to other people, in her desire to satisfy her thirst. Yet our bodies do not really need to be cossetted. Apart from the spiritual gain of self-discipline, there are few people who would not be physically healthier for eating less and plainer food, and the gastric ulcers which plague the present generation would be far less prevalent if we were prepared to miss a meal rather than bolting down an unduly large one at an unfamiliar time to 'make it up.'

But our likes and dislikes apply to many more things than eating and drinking. A love of easy chairs and late lying in bed engenders an attitude of mind which puts comfort higher on our list of personal priorities than our service to God in prayer and worship. Our love of luxuries makes us very often keener to earn money or to decorate our house or to tidy our garden than to devote our time outside reasonable working hours to prayer or reading which will increase our Christian knowledge or devotion. Our health of body frequently engages our attention more pressingly than our health of soul, and even the plea that we are 'under doctor's orders' can become a mere excuse for avoiding unpalatable obligations to God and man.

Nor ought we to forget that there are many essential tasks to be undertaken for the Church in our own town or village which our old way of life may make us reluctant to take up. In our work for the Church, above all, we must guard against the danger of our dislike of having our feelings hurt. Perhaps we have always carried out some particular task for our local Church, or it may be that we feel we should like to undertake a particular job. If we find that we are not required to do it or that we are not thanked for it, we are often hurt beyond measure, and refuse to perform even the tasks we are offered.

Undoubtedly the Church suffers if we behave in such a manner, and we may well derive a certain horrid satisfaction from the feeling that we have been able to get our own back. But it is the damage to our own spiritual life which is really the most grievous aspect of the case. Every attempt to shield our own personality from hurt is a refusal to give of ourselves. Like the hermit crab, we grow soft inside our shell instead of strengthening our fibre by robust and fearless interplay with the world of facts. We are failing in the self-discipline of putting the will of God above our own immediate comfort.

Within the Church we are one of many brethren, for whom it is God's plan that each should perform a function within the whole body. If we demand that things should be done in our way and no-one else's, we are placing our judgment above that of everyone else as to what God wishes. It is fatally easy to stigmatize others as 'un-Christian' and to forget that our own attitude springs from such deep-seated self-love that all charity is driven out, and that there can then be no value in anything we ourselves do.

'If I know all mysteries and all knowledge. . . . and if I bestow all my goods to feed the poor, and if I give my body to be burned, but have not love, it profiteth me nothing,' writes St. Paul to his Corinthian converts.

F

It is we ourselves who lose most in the end!

The Society of the Sacred Mission has a motto that, 'He who is allowed to work for God receives a favour and bestows none.' It is a most searching truth, and a test of all we claim to do for God: do we regard it as a favour we are doing Him, or one which He is doing us? We need to be sufficiently humble to acknowledge with John Milton that, 'God doth not need either man's work or His own gifts.' An insignificant task performed faithfully for the love of Christ is a more precious sacrifice in His sight than some great thing done to satisfy our own self-esteem or to win the admiration of men. To bear uncomplainingly for Christ's sake some hurt or wrong done to us by another is an act of self-denial more acceptable to the crucified Lord than all our zeal for justice and reform.

There is no remedy for the urge to gratify our own desires but to learn through prayer to put our whole trust in God, and to resolve in that spirit a hundred times a day to do things in His way whatever the cost to ourselves. There can be only one right way of doing anything: God's way. Every other way must be wrong.

It follows, then, that we have always to face the actual problems of the next few hours, of the next five minutes, in the unshakable conviction that whatever may be the situation in which we find ourselves, that situation is part of God's purpose, and that God has a purpose for us in that situation.

'Two things are necessary,' says Père de Caussade in one of his letters, 'Firstly the profound conviction that nothing happens in this world, in our souls or outside them, without the design or permission of God; and we ought to submit ourselves no less to what God permits that to what He directly wills; secondly, the firm belief that through the All-powerful and Paternal Providence of

God, all that He wills or permits invariably turns to the advantage of those who practise this submission to His orders. Supported by this double assurance, let us remain firm and unshakable in our adhesion to all that it may please God to ordain with regard to us; let us acquiesce in advance, in a spirit of humility, love and sacrifice in all imaginable dispositions of His providence; let us protest that we wish to be content with whatever satisfies Him.'

This prayer of self-offering is ultimately the highest expression of pure love for God. It depends on complete and fearless trust in Him and in His goodness—a depth of faith which comes easily to no-one, but which we must strive to possess at any expense.

At root, the question is one of relative values. Unless we have that sense of real values in our prayer which enables us to say sincerely to God, 'I know nothing, Thou knowest all things; I am nothing, Thou art everything,' then our prayers will remain no more than an elaborate sham. They will not deceive God, and, being private, they will not deceive our fellow men. But they may easily deceive us, to our great cost. We run the risk of being most strongly opposed to God and firmly separated from Him at the only point at which true contact is possible. We have to learn always and in all things to depend upon God, and to depend upon Him without resentment against either our weakness or His strength.

Have you ever tried to help a sparrow caught in a strawberry net? The bird is quite panic-stricken at its plight, but it is far, far more terrified of the person who comes to its aid! You take it in your hands so very tenderly, and the little heart thuds wildly with terror. Most probably its foot is held by no more than a single thread, but the creature struggles still more madly to escape your handling than it had done to free itself from the net.

The result is quite inevitable: within a few moments it is quite hopelessly entangled, and all your best efforts to free it are frustrated by its desperate fluttering. Exasperated, you take a penknife to the threads and cut the bird free, regretfully ruining your strawberry net in the process.

You can hardly help reflecting how poorly the bird has rewarded your kindness and trouble. Its capture, after all, was its own fault, through an act of flagrant trespass. He came to steal from you, and you have added still further to your loss to obtain his release. Even now, if the country belief is true, the handled bird may die of heartfailure through His own panic, and will not benefit from your pity. Why cannot a bird be more trusting? How much fuss it would save, and how much strawberry netting! He could so easily have been freed if only he would have stayed quiet in your hand. Why could he not understand that your only wish was to help?

But then, are we not equally foolish in God's hand? We become enmeshed in the troubles and anxieties of this world, and we worry and fret until our nerves are tattered. We struggle and panic to resolve the situation, and quite refuse to understand that now, as always, we are in the hand of a loving Father who will beyond all doubt see that we come to no harm.

How we hinder Him by our fretting! We entangle ourselves more fatally all the time He is working to release us. If we would only trust Him, we could be so quickly liberated. Is it likely that God will act less providentially on our behalf than we do for a hapless bird, thief as it is? If we could only learn to be patient, trustful, calm, we should soon be rid of that perpetual worrying which spoils our lives. More important still, we could be immeasurably closer to God and much more truly at His disposal, Whose service is perfect freedom. To have our own way is fatal. To trust in His way leads to eternal life.

This is the essence of the prayer of self-offering: to be always at God's disposal, to be able to say at all times, 'Thy will be done, *by* me and *to* me, what ever the cost.' To pray the words with full sincerity under all circumstances is much more than we are capable of, but it is the aim of all our prayer. Nothing less will do, and nothing but constant and resolute practice in the ways of prayer will make it possible.

10

LIFE IN CHRIST

WE live in an age in which, as in the days of the Old Testament Judges, every man in matters of religion does that which is right in his own eyes. In a sense, the very fact of our freedom of will makes that an essential of human nature in all ages. Yet pride in our own individualism remains the ultimate source of danger to all who tread the steep ascent of prayer. The further we advance, the more we are conscious of our loneliness, for our companions will be fewer at each step we climb. The urge grows steadily to believe that our own comprehension of God is right, and all the other views wrong.

It becomes, then, for us all, the more vitally necessary to keep before our mind, as St. Paul says, that we have nothing which we have not received. If manuals such as this present one have any value as aids to prayer, it is only because they contain something of the teaching which the Church in the person of her saints and doctors has built up and sifted throughout the centuries of her experience of her Lord. When we depart from that teaching, we very readily fall into every sort of error, against which the limited perspective of our own viewpoint offers no adequate defence.

As with the past, so with the present. Our only real hope of continuing a steady ascent towards a knowledge of God lies in our constant intercourse, socially and spiritually, with those who are following the same route. The analogy of the human jig-saw puzzle applies even more cogently to the Church than to the human race as a whole, and the piece which becomes detached from the picture at once ceases to have any true significance.

Biblically, the matter is expressed in the teaching that the Church, the company of the faithful, is the Body of which Christ is the Head. We are the living members, the fingers and thumbs and hands and eyes and ears of the Body. Cut off a finger from a human being and it at once begins to putrify. It is of value only so long as it remains attached and continues to be supplied with the life-giving blood of the body as a whole. Its proper function is seen only when it acts in co-operation with the hand, the arm and the other fingers, without which it cannot so much as lift a pen or flick away a fly.

Still more significantly, the limbs of a body have no purpose which is not controlled by the head. Hands trembling with ague and no longer responsive to the brain are a tragic mockery of their owner, and the wayward, individualistic Christian is no less a source of grief and loss to Christ, the Head of the Body.

Seen in these terms the Church is not a place one goes to, but a Body of which one is an integral part. For the man or woman who prays, their membership of the Church is the indispensable guarantee that their contact with God is real and vital, keyed in to the facts, and not the mere delusion of an individualist. It is, to say the least, unlikely that a faith relying upon unbroken con- tinuity since the time of Abraham, and exercising the best minds and souls of the civilized world for centuries, will be less soundly based on truth than notions which we can conceive for ourselves, or which are of no more than a few centuries' growth.

It is well that we should not forget in our prayers that we are never altogether alone with God. There is with us an innumerable host of heaven, of angels and archangels, of the blessed saints and of the faithful departed; there is also the vast multitude of the faithful at this day, present with us in spirit through their own prayers and through their intercessions for us and for each other. We cannot be (and we should not want to be) Christians on our own, any more than our fingers can be fingers for long if they are cut off from us.

To worship with our fellow-Christians, therefore, is an essential part of our spiritual life. Just as our prayers and adoration contribute to the sum total of that worship, so the Church's common life in Christ flows into and makes alive our own most intimate and private prayer.

Still more important than this, it is only to the members of the Body, *as* members of the Body, that Christ gives His own life. In this lies the whole purpose of the sacrament of the Holy Communion. 'This is my Blood,' said our Blessed Lord, as if He had said, 'This is my Blood which, flowing into your body from the chalice so lovingly offered by Me at the hands of My Church, brings life into each member who receives it as surely as the blood of your own heart brings life to each limb of your own body.'

The aim of our faith is not merely to admire Christ, nor even only to love Him, but to share His own life, to be united with Him inextricably for all eternity. The Blessed Sacrament of the Altar is, as our Book of Common Prayer teaches, the indispensable means by which this unity may be effected here and now, a unity as close and real as that which exists between our own limbs and our own head. Our Lord could not have made the point more emphatically than He did: 'Except ye eat the flesh of the Son of man and drink His blood, *ye have not life in yourselves. He that eateth my flesh and drinketh my blood hath eternal life.*'

In the reception of this Sacrament, then, lies both the

completion and the source of all our life. We cannot hope to pray if we neglect this greatest of all God's gifts, the means by which the Body broken on Calvary and the Blood poured out for us in that most agonizing, redeeming hour, are offered to us for our salvation. At the same time, the gift will remain in us sterile and unavailing if we do not live with God all day and every day in faithful prayer, often explicit, always implicit, arising from a personality gently recollected and continually in the presence of God.

We must stand firm in our belief that prayer is of altogether vital importance, so that we make our prayer-time the very first call upon our day. The less we pray, the less we want to pray, and the harder it is. Make it the first charge upon your time, above everything else. Remember that however badly things may go, there is never a day so bad that it cannot be put right by God through one's prayers. To bring good out of evil presents no difficulty at all to Him. At the same time there is no day so good that it will not be spoiled if it is not brought to Him.

Prayer for the Christian is like the magic touch of King Midas—it turns all else to the purest gold. It gives the soul wings which lift it up to God. It puts into the hand of God a cord with which He will bind us to Himself for all eternity.

APPENDIX

FOR those who find a mnemonic useful, the following summary of the five 'modes' or 'parts' of prayer is given, with chapter references from the text of the book:

> **P**enitence—(Chapter 4)
> **A**doration (praise)—(Chapter 8)
> **R**equests (petition and intercession)—(Chapter 3)
> **T**hanksgiving—(Chapter 8)
> **S**elf-offering—(Chapter 9)

It is not suggested that one should pray by working systematically through these PARTS of prayer unless one happens personally to find this useful. The mnemonic is intended simply as an aid to prayer at those times when one 'seems to have nothing to say', as a reminder of what *can* be said or done in prayer time.

Sooner or later all five parts must find their place in our prayers, but the balance between them will necessarily change profoundly from time to time. Of course, any one of these parts can become the subject of mental prayer.